Coming of age Gracefully

Foreword

Aging is a lifelong journey. A journey filled with laughter, hurt, love, dreams, pain, anxiety and joy. It is a journey in which we experience many changes and challenges along the way.

Signs of age...gray hair, a wrinkled brow...are signs of change. Change that is inevitable in this never-ending journey we call life. These changes...these experiences help us grow and shape the person we are and will become. They help us gain the special wisdom that can only come with age.

This wisdom is a gift from God. A gift to be shared with and treasured by those of a younger generation.

Coming of Age Gracefully captures the essence of the lifelong journey of aging. We have asked well-known theologians, scholars and others to share the experiences, anecdotes and wisdom that have shaped their lives...and helped them learn the lessons that only life itself can teach. We have also reprinted special writings from actors, authors and famous individuals which reflect their life experiences...and their thoughts on the aging process. We are reminded that, regardless of our place in life—how well-known or wealthy we are—we all age...we all experience...we all must face the inevitable changes that life casts upon us.

These authors demonstrate that it is possible to age gracefully and with dignity. They offer encouragement to prosper in the face of limitation or loss. And, they help us realize that aging is a lifelong process...a time filled with hope, joy and opportunity. Their struggles, triumphs and insights are truly an inspiration to all of us. For aging is a journey in which we all must partake. Our struggles, joys, visions and fears are shared by others...in age, we are not alone. The writings you will find in *Coming of Age Gracefully* are truly writings from the heart...to the heart.

It is hoped that as you read *Coming of Age Gracefully*, you will reflect on your own life's journey. You may be moved to record your thoughts in a journal, or to simply discuss them with those close to you. You have the opportunity to give the gift of comfort to others through your words and wisdom.

We hope you enjoy *Coming of Age Gracefully*...a benefit created exclusively for AAL members.

Aid Association for Lutherans

Table of Contents

Coming of Age Gracefully
© 1995 Aid Association for Lutherans

Coming of age Gracefully

Being and Becoming

From the moment we are born, our experiences shape the person we are...and lay the foundation for the person we will become.

Becoming is a never-ending process...a process of experimenting...experiencing...growing...and most of all, it is a realization that, in life, change is inevitable.

In short, becoming is learning how to live.

Learning how to live means accepting changes as opportunities. It means realizing that as much as we plan, life just can't be in a neat little box. Learning how to live means seeing the world through the eyes of others...seeking new challenges and using our abilities to their fullest. And most of all, it means learning how to see the good in ourselves and others.

Throughout our lives, we play many roles. We are mothers, brothers, stock brokers, neighbors, housewives, plumbers, farmers, friends...yet, these are merely roles that provide us with the learning experiences that enable us to become.

This section is a celebration of these experiences... the uniqueness...that is within each of us...an appreciation of what we are and a celebration of what we're becoming.

"Not that I have already attained all this, or have already been made perfect, but I press on to take hold of that for which Christ Jesus took hold of me."

Philippians 3:12 NIV

Creativity: A Fresh Approach to Aging

Rollo May

I think the later years ought to be the time when we enjoy the creativity that we have.

I feel very strongly that creativity keeps us fresh, even though it requires great discipline and struggle. Fresh is the word I use, not young. I don't see becoming young as desirable at all, because young people often don't have the creativity that we have as we grow older. Creativity keeps us fresh; it keeps us alive, keeps us moving forward. I think the older we get, the fresher we ought to get. We face our fears. We tackle them head on. We have the courage to create.

I really think creativity is the answer to aging, and by creativity I mean listening to one's own inner voice, to one's own ideas, to one's own aspirations. It may be social work. It may be gardening. It may be building. But it must be something fresh, something new, some idea that takes fire — this is what I'd like to see among older people. When Matisse was in bed and couldn't get up the last year of his life, he found something creative to do. He got himself a pair of scissors and made all these cutouts in paper, and they are fan-tastically beautiful. I love them very much. I have a reproduction of one in my office, leaning up against one of the walls to remind me of what old people can do in their last years.

I believe that one lives as long as one has something to con-tribute. All the creative people that I've known have died once they stopped being creative.

Now, I may have the cart before the horse there — they may have stopped their creativity because they sensed that some-thing was being blocked — but I have this prejudice that we live so long as we have something impor-tant to say. Once we've said it, we die. Kierkegaard died in his middle forties, but he said what he needed to say. Pascal died in his late fifties, but he said what he needed to say. So I don't know that time is so crucial in this matter of death. Does it make a difference whether you die in your thirties or in your eighties? It seems to me you ought to judge these things not by the number of years somebody lived, but by the concept of eternity.

*"It's not what you were,
it's what you are today."*

David Marion

A Change for the Better

Charles Arn

It has been my privilege to study men and women in our country who have lived long, productive, satisfying lives. My mission? To find out what qualities these people share in common.

One of the things I have found is that older adults who "live long and love it" have learned to cope with change. These are people who have determined that dealing with the changes we face in life is simply better than stagnation. In short, they look at changes as opportunities for growth.

What kinds of changes do these people — and all of us — encounter? Everything from the death of a spouse or close family member, marital separation, loss of a job, trouble with a boss, change in social activities to minor physical problems to name just a few.

Of course, in addition to the events themselves, come the changes that such events precipitate. The loss of a loved one, the discovery of a life-threatening disease — these are painful transitions in life. Such changes, whether they happen to us or to those around us, put a lump in our throat, a tear on our cheek.

I would like to share with you four insights I have learned from those older adults who have learned how to make change work for them.

1. Count your blessings. My sister has a friend with cerebral palsy. She spends most of her waking hours in a wheel chair. She has problems with coordination, vision and speech. But she just completed her bachelor of arts degree summa cum laude, and is optimistically looking for a job. She told me the other day, "I'm luckier than a lot of people." When change happens to you — and it will — remember the things you do have and count your blessings.

2. Focus on the long term. What seems unbearable today will, in time, become manageable. Time is truly a great healer. One of my favorite songs ends with the phrase, "The darkest hour means dawn is just in sight."

3. Keep searching for the good. We've all heard the question, "Is your cup half full or half empty?" People whose cup is half full seem better able to

handle change. Maintain a positive mental attitude.

4. Get out of yourself. The more we think about ourselves and our own problems, the more unhappy we become. Often the best approach to handling change is to spend our time and energy helping someone else. In losing ourselves in a greater cause, we can actually find ourselves.

Change is part of our human experience. It always will be. Some people see change as an unwanted intrusion in life. Such people respond to change with anger, fear, annoyance or retreat.

Others, however, focus on the future, and see their new situation through optimistic eyes of expectation. Change often begins a wonderful new part of their lives. The same event, for these people with positive attitudes, becomes an opportunity to grow and expand.

The following poem wonderfully illustrates the difference in how people respond to change as they move through life's journey...

The covered wagon rolled and pitched
along the prairie track.
One sat looking forward,
while one sat looking back.

One scanned the vast horizon
for a bright and better day.
While the other watched the fading road,
'til it, too, slipped away.

The covered wagon rolled and pitched
along the prairie track.
One sat looking forward,
while one sat looking back.

author unknown

Having Our Say: The Delany Sisters' First 100 Years

Sarah Louise and Annie Elizabeth Delany

Bessie and I have been together since time began, or so it seems. Bessie is my little sister, only she's not so little.

She is 101 years old, and I am 103. People always say they'd like to live to be one hundred, but no one really expects to, except Bessie. She always said she planned to be as old as Moses. And when Bessie says she's going to do something, she does it. Now, I think Moses lived to 120. So I told Bessie that if she lives to 120, then I'll just have to live to 122 so I can take care of her.

Neither one of us ever married and we've lived together most all of our lives, and probably know each other better than any two human beings on this Earth. After so long, we are in some ways like one person. She is my right arm. If she were to die first, I'm not sure if I would want to go on living because the reason I am living is to keep her living.

We've buried so many people we've loved; that is the hard part of living this long. Most everyone we know has turned to dust. Well, there must be some reason we're still here. That's why we agreed to do this book; it gives us a sense of purpose. If it helps just one person, then it's worth doing. That's what Mama used to say.

There's a few things I have had to give up. I gave up driving a while back. I guess I was in my late eighties. That was terrible. Another thing I gave up on was cutting back my trees so we have a view of the New York City skyline to the south. Until I was ninety-eight years old, I would climb up on the ladder and saw those tree branches off so we had a view. I could do it perfectly well; why pay somebody to do it? Then Sadie talked some sense into me, and I gave up doing it.

The Delany Sisters (left to right), Sarah, 103, Bessie, 101.

It's hard being old, because you can't always do everything you want, exactly as you want it done. When you get as old as we are, you have to struggle to hang onto your freedom, your independence. We have a lot of family and friends keeping an eye on us, but we try not to be dependent on any one person. We try to pay people, even relatives, for whatever they buy for us, and for gasoline for their car, things like that, so that we do not feel beholden to them.

Truth is, I never thought I'd see the day when people would be interested in hearing what two old Negro women have to say. Life still surprises me. So maybe the last laugh's on me.

Photograph by Brian Douglas from HAVING OUR SAY: The Delany Sister's First 100 Years by Sarah and A. Elizabeth Delany with Amy Hill Hearth. Published in 1994 by Kodansha America, Inc. Copyright ©1994 by Sarah Louise Delany, Annie Elizabeth Delany and Amy Hill Hearth.

The Art of Being

James P. Schaefer

I was fresh out of seminary when I met Art. He was the president of the congregation I had been assigned to serve. To this day, I have met few people who had a better insight into the workings of the mind. Art was a great talker. But the best part about Art was that there was no gap between what he said and how he lived. He walked his talk.

Art was not a person whose life had no center. He was a fully integrated person whose life was centered in his Lord and surrounded by a personality which he accepted without apology. Like all of us, he had his faults, but they never shook that rock-solid center around which he had built his life.

Art was also a businessman. And, an astute one, at that. Though customers may not have cared for his product or prices, they never questioned his integrity.

Not long after I left the congregation, Art came to one of those crossroads in life that we all dread.

Art in the '70s

For health reasons, he was forced to give up his business. He was several years from retirement and I worried about his future. I need not have. Within weeks, he had bought another business and within a year or two, it became more prosperous than the business he had left. Art was moving on without a backward glance, firmly believing that God was at the center, holding his life together.

Although Art died some years ago, he still stands before me. Tall and strong, with a character cast in concrete. He had most of the characteristics we admire in people. Without complaint, he rose to meet the challenges of his life.

Art bequeathed to me an invaluable gift: he taught me how to live.

The lessons I learned from Art were those that years of traditional professors and classrooms couldn't possibly teach me. Because the beauty in life for Art was in giving, not getting. He was a generous person.

Never too busy to help a little boy repair his bicycle, to speak a word of encouragement to a friend or to help a neighbor. But he had no time to be a cynic, to put someone down, to spread ugly gossip or to hurt another person.

Thankfully for all of us, God has sprinkled this world with Arts. And — thank God — there is a little of Art in all of us. The Arts of the world teach us that lives do have meaning. That lives are for reaching out.

I learned so much from Art, I thought I'd share a little bit of him with you. He rarely "lectured." He taught by example. I hope these few words about Art will lift your spirits, make your day a little brighter, and encourage you to attend more closely to the Art that God has placed in your heart. Arise and shine! Art is beckoning you, too!

Stir It Up

Marty Knowlton

I like being an old guy. I'm much more secure in who I am. There's been just huge amounts of thrashing in my life, but I've learned to reflect on them, to learn from them. You know, there's no way that one can ever change the past. So when I talk about having lived through unsatisfactory and disturbing episodes in my past, there's nothing I can do about those things. All I can do is understand myself and recognize that virtually all of the bad things that have happened to me in my life, as far as I know, were things that I could have changed. As long as I keep recognizing that, it's useful to me because I'm now less ready to hide myself behind circumstances and say, "Well, I can't do this for this reason or that reason." I usually know where responsibility lies now, and I'm much more ready to act in a responsible fashion than I have been. I'm growing up. But if regrets were snowflakes I'd be buried right now. As a matter of fact, they might have even formed a glacier by this time.

I really think that I'm more strongly in touch with the realities and much more deeply in touch with the unrealities as an old man. Many of my sensations of living are almost blindingly vivid now. I love being alive at age seventy-one. I anticipate loving it just as much, maybe better, at seventy-

two. I describe my function today as "stirring things up." Now, it isn't something that I do consciously, and I try to be cautious when I realize that I'm being disruptive — I don't want to send somebody into hysterics or anything like that. But on the other hand, I'm perfectly pleased with myself when I have the sense that I have stirred things up; that's living. If you're not stirred up, you're not really living. Elders need a certain amount of discomfort to really live; they need irritation, okay? They need to be indignant about things.

This Changing House

ging is a lifelong journey. A journey with no clear beginning and no clear end. Yet, there are signs along the way.

We notice a few gray hairs. Wrinkles begin to show as our faces become more seasoned and worn with time. We do things just a little more slowly than we once did. Maybe we put on a few pounds we just can't seem to shake. These, of course, are the more obvious, physical changes we encounter along our journey.

But life's journey takes us beyond the obvious, physical changes of aging. It reaches deep within each of us.

Through it all, we come to realize that aging can be a beautiful journey...a transformation into a world where outward appearance is secondary to a far more endearing inner beauty and strength. While the physical appearance of our youth may be long gone, we never lose our capacity to love, to experience, to share, to enjoy.

Come, let us continue the journey...

"We do not lose heart. Though outwardly we are wasting away, yet inwardly we are being renewed day by day."

2 Corinthians 4:16 NIV

The Touch of Life

Herb Brokering

They did not talk about it. But they both knew about it. Their need to touch. It was there from the beginning. They did not take it for granted. It was their great gift to each other. Their lives were opened as they grew in love by touching.

They touched accidentally... they touched on purpose. They stayed in touch, by touching. He called her his Oak, a tree that would withstand a storm... a firm tree with deep roots. When they lay under a favorite tree, on a summer day, looking up, he reached to hold her and

whisper: You are the Oak. She received his touch, and his word. Something deep inside flowed between them; they knew it was love.

He sometimes called her his Violet. Then he touched her more gently, and spoke more softly. He felt her fragile spirit. The words Violet and Oak went deeper than skin. They stirred a picture deep inside their minds. They were communicating inside out.

Sometimes she looked into his eyes. She saw a world she wished to know more about. She knew him well, but there

was even more. She wanted to be in there where he was most alive, most unique, most in love. And he wanted all this of her. They did not discuss this look between them. They enjoyed it and gave it to the other. They were in touch, deep inside.

Through the years, their bodies gradually changed. But they had memorized each other through time and touch. Years only added to the volume of their touches. Years did not change what they saw and felt and knew with closed eyes. Deep in their minds they touched, and what they saw was there from the first time.

They remember the many ways both reached out to touch. A rose or carnation, a card with a perfect verse, a favorite place, a special dessert, a surprise, a gift they could not afford, a trip they did not expect, a chosen word. They remember a sigh of relief, just being there, perfect silence, a squeeze, a nod of support, a hug from behind, a balloon, perfume, a first bloom from the garden.

They have grown so together. He knows her needs and wants. He knows just where the Oak stands.

Years have passed. They walk slower, but inside they are the same. Others from their early life do not recognize them. Yet, they keep knowing one another. Their bodies have changed, but when they touch they know it is the other. They recognize the Oak, the Violet, the silk dress, the cotton shirt, the hug, the twinkle.

What they have always known is still true. People increase in love and understanding through touch. Touch increases life. Touch is medicine.

When they reach out to touch each other, the earth, the wind, a friend—the mind feeds the body a flow of healing. Touching stirs new life in them. Now, he does what he never had time to do. She knits more. He marvels as seasons come and go. They do not watch the clock as much as then. He was always on time. Time is bigger now. Now contains all the times of their years.

They are very wealthy, the people say. Midas wished that all he touched would turn to gold. What they touch turns into love and life.

Inside all of us is the need to touch. It is a source of life.

At Seventy: A Journal

May Sarton

Why do we worry about lines in our faces as we grow old? A face without lines that shows no mark of what has been lived through in a long life suggests something unlived, empty, behind it....

Still, one mourns one's young face sometimes. It has to be admitted. I now use a night cream for the first time in my life. At the same time, as I went over photographs yesterday for a children's book of biographies in which I am included, I felt that my face is better now, and I like it better. That is because I am a far more complete and richer person than I was at twenty-five, when ambition and personal conflicts were paramount and there was a surface of sophistication that was not true of the person inside.

Now I wear the inside person outside and am more comfortable with my self. In some ways I am younger because I can admit vulnerability and more innocent because I do not have to pretend.

An Intimate Conversation with Art Linkletter

Dr. Richard Besdine, Director of the Aging Center, University of Connecticut, said in TIME Magazine: "Aging doesn't necessarily mean a life that is sick, senile or sexless."

I support that thinking. I'm over 80 and I'm in the prime of life. I just need a little longer to get primed.

When we think of the "later years," do we think of memory loss, wrinkles, loneliness, depression, indigestion, painful joints and loss of our sex life? Are we to meekly accept all of these? No!

Most of the problems are not "natural" results of aging. Rather, they generally come from stress, poor health habits and illness associated with smoking, alcohol abuse, a diet high in fat and just plain inactivity.

Our sexuality can be threatened by many of these physical problems, but the chief culprit is quite often the attitude and self-esteem of an older person. Our mental attitude toward intimacy provides the focus for meaningful relationships that deepen with an understanding of and commitment to each other.

For most older people the "coals are still warm," even if the fire's been dampened by loss of relationships and the perceived disapproval of family and friends. But, don't buy the notion that we older adults are supposed to be sexless. Research shows that people have the capacity for active sexual expression well into their nineties. And if we choose, chances are very good that we can still experience that God-given expression of ourselves to others.

Almost every doctor thinks sexual expression is good for older people. They tell us it's good for our general physiology and that it takes place the way it always did when we were younger. The only problem is that according to many expert clinical psychologists, some doctors refuse to open the subject with their older patients. And that's a shame because there's a lot they could do to help as we strive to continue this important expression in our lives.

Older Americans have the right to be attracted to others, just as they always were. Sexual dysfunction isn't something that occurs automatically when one passes a certain age. Sexuality, which includes looking good, dressing well and appearing attractive to the opposite sex, is important to healthy older adults. As one clinical psychologist said, "It's the last thing to go."

Regardless of how far we think we've come in the twentieth century in addressing certain subjects, "sex" is one that still is considered, by much of society, as "not nice" after a certain age (whatever that may be). And there are reasons for that. When an older parent dies, children often feel that a mother or father cannot be replaced, which may result in misguided and unrealistic attitudes towards the surviving parent. Older children may be concerned that if a parent remarries, their inheritance may be affected. Others may have unrealistic expectations of the need for intimacy for the surviving parent, which foster inaccurate assumptions. As one younger woman said when asked about her widowed mother and sex, "Oh no. I know my mother wouldn't, but my mother-in-law would!"

The subject of sexuality among older Americans is generally not openly discussed. Nevertheless, there are a few points I'd like to make. When people marry in later years, intimacy can stop at a level that doesn't include sexual intimacy—particularly if the primary objective for marrying is companionship. Of course, medical problems may affect sexual desire and the increased number of medications older Americans may take can also be a factor. If there is a problem, a doctor may be able to help, but in order to help, the doctor has to be informed about the problem. As I stated earlier, some physicians, particularly if they're younger than their patients, may not open the subject of sexual intimacy with their older patients.

Experts say, whatever one's sexual practices have been before, the same expectations and desires continue in later years. Simply stated, if sexual intimacy has been an important part of our lives, it is normal to want it to continue. The choice continues to be ours.

Our physical, spiritual, emotional, intellectual selves define who we are. Let's keep these in balance throughout our lives. I'm all for it!

You tell me I'm getting old,
You just don't understand.
The dweller in my house
Is young and bright and gay,
Just starting on a life to last
Throughout eternal day.
You only see the outside
Which is all most folks see.
You tell me I'm getting old,
You've mixed my house with me!

author unknown

The Autumn of My Life

Polly Francis

What a baffling thing old age is! It doesn't bring the peace we were led to expect. I find it hard to drift with the stream; all along the way there are problems which obstruct the smooth flow of life. The area which lies between the "here" and the "hereafter" is a difficult passage to travel. One must make the journey to fully understand it.

The young people may think that we are unreasonably demanding. It seems to them that all our needs are met. We are comfortably housed, well fed, protected from hazards, provided with companionship and amusements. What else do we need?

Our greatest need is not met. It is one that we never outgrow. It is the need to feel cherished by someone—to know that there is a place where we "belong." This is something that no retirement home, nursing home or hospital can provide. These institutions are staffed by dedicated people, but it is not their function to soothe our yearning hearts.

Age creeps up so stealthily that it is often with shock that we become aware of its presence. Perhaps that is why so many of us reach old age utterly unprepared to meet its demands. We may be a bit rebellious about accepting it; I want to cry out that the invisible part of me is not old. I still thrill to the beauties of the world—the dew upon the rose at dawn, the glow reflected by the sun on passing cloud when day is done—but unremitting age goes on.

When my courage turns limp, I ponder my past. I try to find a yardstick with which to measure the merit of a life. I become so confused that I cannot tell right from wrong. They come so close together and dance so fast from side to side that I am unable to grasp them firmly. And that is where faith comes in. We cannot know; we can only believe.

Old age is not all pain and limitations. It holds its own joys and satisfactions. The time has come when musing replaces activities—when the sleepless hours are filled from the harvest of a well-stored mind. Even though our means are scant, we know that our material needs will, somehow, be met. But an impoverished soul is a saddening thing.

The common expression, "so-and-so is failing," is tossed around too freely. In aging we gain as well as lose. The autumn of human life, like the autumn of nature, can bring richness of beauty. It's a time when our spiritual forces seem to expand. A life of the heart and of the mind takes over while our physical force ebbs away.

"You can take no credit for beauty at sixteen. But if you are beautiful at sixty, it will be your own soul's doing."

Marie Carmichael Stopes

Letting Go...Moving On

ife is a series of transitions. Some easier than others. How we adjust to these changes goes a long way toward shaping who we are, what we get out of life and what we give to life.

Some changes we bring on ourselves. We marry. We take new jobs. We meet new people. Some are not of our own choosing. The death of a loved one. Physical limitation. Financial hardship. And still others are just a natural progression of life itself. Retirement, children leaving home, ending of relationships.

Change means letting go of the past that has helped to define our lives. And, it means confronting the range of emotions...the pain, anxiety, joy, sorrow...that make change a uniquely human experience.

Change challenges us to draw on an inner strength...a strength we become more acutely aware of as we age. For it is after we have lived...experienced...endured...that we realize that change is inevitable...and that sometimes, letting go is not an end, but rather, a beginning.

"Through many dangers, toils and snares I have already come. 'Tis grace has brought me safe thus far, and grace will lead me home."

John Newton, 1725-1807

Precious Memories

Karl Lutze

I am embarrassed—no, ashamed—that I asked the question.

Albert and Charlotte were moving from Illinois to Virginia. It was a traumatic moment for them. Their children were all grown and had left the nest. The day of retirement had come, and these two dear friends were embarking on a new chapter in their lives.

It's never easy to move. What is probably hardest comes with choosing what to take along and what to throw out—or to give away. There's bound to be some debate.

The husband wonders why in the world his wife insists on keeping all those absolutely "useless" things she's been keeping on the top shelf of her closet. And when his wife is pitching into a large green plastic bag things that have been lying in the very back of her husband's desk drawers for over forty years, he shouts from the next room, "Don't you dare throw that away—I plan to use it sometime!"

After much debate, they loaded their things into the moving van, said goodbye to their neighbors, took a long and final nostalgic look at familiar surroundings and with lumps in their throats, and tears in their eyes, they headed for Virginia.

With a late start, and already wearied from the ordeal, they chose to travel only a portion of the way so they might get a good night's rest with a sister who happened to be our next door neighbor.

Just as they were settling back in their chairs to catch their breaths and take advantage of some much needed relaxation, the terrible phone call came. The moving van carrying all their belongings had caught fire and everything—*everything*—had gone up in flames.

When I learned what had happened, I went to see them and that's when I asked the extremely inappropriate question, "Was it covered by insurance?"

In tears and anger—but in kind words for me—Al explained, "It's not dollars and cents! It's the family piano around which we would gather and sing hymns and the Christmas carols. It's the table around which we'd sit and pray and eat and laugh and talk over what was happening in our lives. It's the beds next to which we'd kneel and pray with the children."

What he was really saying was that "things" aren't really valuable except as they remind us of certain persons who have special significance for us. In the end, one of my most embarrassing moments helped to teach me one of life's most valuable lessons.

The day may come when we ourselves may have to move into smaller quarters because the old house is just too big to care for. If, at that time, we are limited in what we take with us, it may prove wise not to take along the most expensive items, but rather, those that conjure up for us the warmest and most beautiful memories of people who have enriched our lives, who've meant the most to us, who've brought us great happiness.

In assessing the value of the various possessions God has given us, we do well to prize as particularly precious the greatest gift of all—the gift that God has given to each of us in that moment when a fragment of bread and a sip of wine are ours to see and feel and taste as we are told about the One who "let go" of everything because he would not let go of us.

FREE

Elise Maclay

I hate to admit it,
But I'm glad the children aren't babies anymore.
I adored it when they were.
I honestly never felt tied down, I
Wanted them with me wherever I went.
They defined me. They meant
I had a purpose in life
I was
A mother.
Other women had a child or two in tow,
It seemed, everywhere I looked,
Mothers and children.
I wanted to be part of that universe
And I was.
It was a sensual thing, too,
I loved the feel of chubby arms around my neck.
I needed
The clutch of their need.
We agreed before we married
That children were what marriage was about,
And it worked out.

We were a family.
We did things together,
As a family, picnics, Little League,
No dancing till dawn,
No trips to Capri,
But I never minded,
Never envied childless couples,
Was always glad to be
Me.
Amazingly I still am.
Glad to be a grandmother?
Yes. I confess
It hasn't much to do with
The grandchildren. They
Live pretty far away.
No, what I'm saying is that
It's unexpectedly delicious
To be free,
To go anywhere at the drop of a hat,
No calls to sitters,
To be able to stay away overnight,
Change my plans,
Dawdle, wander. I used to be
So rushed, in a library, in a bookstore,
Now I can linger.

I take binoculars whenever I go out in the car,
In case I pass a marsh or field good for
Bird-watching. I stop in and visit friends,
And go along with them if they invite me.
I park at scenic overlooks and look over.
Hardly anyone who lives here does.
I watch construction,
I see people staring at me with pity,
I imagine they say, That poor old woman
With nothing to do all day.
It's hard not to grin, because
I feel like Huckleberry Finn.

Dear Teri

Judy Green Herbstreit

This is a letter written from mother to daughter in late 1979.

Dear Teri,

It is difficult to grow up. It is very difficult to leave your home. It is not only hard on you, but on your family.

Children are a mixed blessing. They are a tremendous source of work, time spent, money invested, pain, joy, sadness, pride, closeness. You often wonder if they understand—or care—about the things you give them while you do with-out—the nights you bake all night to give them happy memories—the fears you have for them because they do refuse to understand that life is not really going to be a "take" situation when they get out in it—as it is now while they are safe in the growing years.

Remember the saying I used to keep on the refrigerator? "A mother is not a person to lean on but a person to make leaning unnecessary."

When the day comes for your child to leave home, you want them to be able to say, "Mom, I'm ready! I can do it, Mom! I'm going to fly on my own."

You are ready to go, Teri. I assure you you can fly. It is time for you to do it.

You have mountains to climb—without me. I don't even know your world, I don't know your mountains.

You have my love. You have my support and my encouragement. (I cheer good.) You have me believing you can do what you want to do—whatever it is. That's all I can give you now. I've done the best I could do as your mother. I know I've failed you sometimes, it is unavoidable in raising a human being—especially when you are only a human being yourself, and you are still climbing your own mountains.

The best thing you can do is believe in yourself. Don't be afraid to try. Don't be afraid to fail. Just try again. Just dust yourself off and try again.

The last important thing to remember is: Philippians 4:13, "I can do all things through Christ who strengthens me."

My love and thoughts go with you. My first child. My daughter.

Love, MOM

"I can do all things through Christ who strengthens me."

Philippians 4:13

Losses in Later Life

R. Scott Sullender

We used to think of ourselves as a young person with all of the trappings that go with youth. Then that image of ourselves gets stripped away as we pass into later adulthood. We used to take some comfort in thinking of ourselves as a son or daughter—but when our parents become ill and die, we realize that we can never go home again. We used to think of ourselves as a worker, a tradesperson or a professional in some line of work—but in retirement that self-definition gets stripped way. We used to think of ourselves as a husband, a wife, a lover, a partner—but that role is stripped from us in the anguish of our spouse's death. Eventually, we cannot even think of ourselves as a whole person, a healthy person, an independent person. We must yet again redefine ourselves. One after another, our identities are stripped away.

This "stripping away" process can also be an opportunity to discover a deeper understanding of ourselves, a core identity, that perhaps transcends all of our former identities. Here are a few

segments from a series of conversations I had with a wonderful older gentleman whom I had asked to reflect on the process of aging in later life.

"During the last twenty years of my life I have felt somewhat like an onion. One layer after another has been stripped way from me. First my career went. Then, my beloved wife, Bea. Then, my mobility. At least I still have my writing. I do love to write, mostly little things for the local newspaper. But I expect that in time that will go. My eyes will fail or something. I wonder, sometimes, what will be left of me. What is the core of the onion really like?

"When each layer of the onion goes, a part of me goes. There's a lot of hurt in old age. Everything that is important to you is taken away, one by one. And this is how it is for many people in old age.

"The wonderful thing about this process is that each time I redefine myself I come up with a better definition. Each time I come to see myself in a more profound way. Each time I

reach a little deeper into my soul. I become more of who I really am. Now, at seventy-five, I think I know myself better than I ever have in my life. I have come to see myself, I think for the first time, for what I really am. My real essence is here (points to his heart). It's not in what I did, or in my children, or in my accomplishments—no, it's in what I am, in here. This is a real me (points to his heart) and it's taken me seventy-five years to get down to it."

Life in the later years is essentially a spiritual journey precisely because the loss process forces us more and more to focus on and value our spiritual selves. There is, therefore, great potential for spiritual growth and renewal in and through the loss of identity.

Dream On

Jo Horne

Even though we may not be able to accomplish all our life's dreams, we always have a mission no matter what our age.

Every child has a dream... to play basketball like Michael Jordan, to win an Olympic gold medal, to make a gazillion dollars so you can buy anything you want. Come to think of it, at any given time, most adults have a dream or two up their sleeves, too. Dreams make getting through the work week a little easier...they help us get through the difficult days. Most often, dreams are framed in terms of maybe...perhaps... someday...if only....

We've all been there. Someday I'm going to write that book, paint that picture, get that degree, start my own business. If only I had the time (the money, the talent, the education) I would _____ (you fill in the blank). Perhaps after I retire, I'll _____. Someday....

And what happens to most of us? The years go by and while some of our goals and dreams are fulfilled, we wind up postponing or revamping or discarding others altogether.

We move on. Life is busy...full...demanding.

It's important, however, that as we move through life— and especially when we find ourselves coming to the end of certain responsibilities—(work, parenting, etc.) that we hold onto our dreams.

In fact, these are the times when we should all indulge ourselves a bit...contemplate the possibilities...put aside any idea that we might be "too old" for such foolishness.

Think about President Carter's mom, Lillian, who fulfilled her dream and headed off to the Peace Corps when she was in her seventies. Of course, you don't have to be famous (or the mother of someone famous) to live out a dream.

But, there is the issue of reality. Sure, it may be unrealistic to think of becoming a best selling author...but what about taking some writing or language classes? Contributing a piece or two to some local paper or magazine?

And speaking of classes, perhaps you'll never get your

doctorate, but if you've always dreamed of finishing that bachelor's degree, go for it. What better time? Most colleges have reduced tuition rates for older adults.

There may never be a better time for pursuing dreams than in our later years. There's nothing more rewarding in life than doing something you love and having it make a real difference... however small. Now, we're not talking Academy Awards or Medal of Honor here. This is

about finding something you love, that you've always wanted to try and just doing it. Or take something you do well and turn it into something that can make a difference for others. And if you think you have nothing to give, take a look at the world around you...and think again.

One of the issues that tends to haunt people as they grow older is what meaning has their life had...what will they be remembered for?

In his last years, I remember my father fretting about what he had left for his children. As a businessman, he, of course, was talking about financial security. But I knew there was something he had given to me that was far more priceless than any trust fund or bank account.

I had watched him all my life, seen him change directions a dozen times or more, seen him find the time for the things that were dear to him...his family, his church, his community, his work. But I had also seen him take time for himself...find pleasure in the woodworking that allowed him hours alone to think and turn a plain piece of wood into a model ship or a piece of doll furniture. He did it not to win prizes or make money, but simply because it gave him pleasure.

The legacy my father gave me was the belief that all things were possible...and the understanding that sometimes the satisfaction is to be found in the attempt.

Working Beyond Work

hy does the word "retirement" stir up so many and such mixed emotions? For some, the word retirement signals an end. For others, it marks a much anticipated beginning.

Perhaps the anxiety over retirement is that unfortunately, we too often confuse what a person "does" with what he or she actually "is."

We are accountants, electricians, social workers, nurses, farmers, business people, housewives. But the beauty of retirement is that as we shed those roles, we free ourselves to experience, express and live beyond those roles that have shaped our lives for so many years.

Retirement, then, is essentially a rebirth. A time to explore new interests, to forge new relationships and to seek out new experiences.

> "By the grace of God I am what I am."
>
> 1 Corinthians 15:10 NIV

As we shed our "working" personas, we realize that beneath the suits, inside the aprons, behind the coveralls and steel-toed boots, we are more than simply members of a working group.

We are individuals with unique perspectives...eager to learn...to grow... to stimulate the senses and excite the mind in ways that have been put aside during our working years. It is upon retirement that we have the freedom to discover those things we truly value in life...and to seek out the inner tranquility and harmony that makes life complete.

These are truly the expressions of life. Expressions of freedom and of the joy that come with achieving harmony with nature, God, ourselves and others. As we strive toward complete harmony and inner peace, our work bears fruit and our lives become whole.

Reflections

Gracia Grindal

Experts say that the first decade after retirement is the time when many of us still have the ability to do some of the things we have longed to do while working: travel, read, garden, golf, write a novel, start new hobbies, explore new interests and get to know our grandchildren. Some of us, however, may find it hard to think of such activities as being "useful".

Some people who have reached retirement age remark on how much time "retirement" actually takes. Caught up in all these activities, they feel just as busy as they did when they were working. Some like it. Some don't. Why? Because they do not feel useful. There are, however, many kinds of uses for one's gifts.

Retirement may be a time in which one has a chance, at last, to devote time to helping the community: teaching young children, helping those in need, restoring old buildings, building new ones, helping to make the useful arts flourish among us. But it is not just activities that help to give our lives value.

We can all enjoy one explicit pleasure of old age, that is the chance to reflect over a long time. And that is precisely why the newly retired have so much to give: they are wise, they have stored up years of reflection on the human condition, and they are therefore drawn toward others with a desire to help and serve them while they still are able.

These years of reflection are not necessarily scholarly, though they can be. These reflections on life—memories, really—can be enjoyed like a ripe pear in late autumn with its dusky scent of summer filling the room. For the same reason grandchildren revere their grandparents: they love that ripe, musky wisdom about who they are as told by someone who knows them and loves them.

Memory is useful. It can tell younger generations what is dangerous and what is good. That's why recently retired people can be so vital to have help with projects. They remember how things are, they know how to do things, how to live and work with human beings. The history of the world is in their hands and they pass on their wisdom to the young. Retired people are a national treasure. For they have something the society needs: wisdom.

The wonderful thing about all human life is that it is never too late to start, despite one's regret. For it is in retirement, if health allows, when freedom is a gift to each of us.

Living Harmony

Tom Droege

If we thought of the times in our lives when we felt a deep sense of living in harmony with nature, God, ourselves and others, when would those times be? A particular day, hour or moment when everything seemed balanced and ordered? Perhaps it was a longer time; a courtship, a honeymoon or an entire marriage in which love has grown more deeply with each passing year. One such time remains vivid in my memory.

When I was 20, I spent the summer working for the U.S. Forestry Service in upper Idaho and lived in a tent camp miles from civilization. My daily task was a lonely one; eradicate a bush that transmitted disease from one white pine to another. Alone, I worked the slopes of pristine pine-forested mountains. I soon discovered the forest was alive with fellow creatures and suffused with the presence of God. He began speaking to me, and I began listening.

One day I entered a clearing high on the mountain. There, before me, stretched a magnificent view of pine forests as far as the eye could see. For a time, I stood in wonder, suspended between two worlds, on the edge of mystery in the near presence of God. Then it happened. Slowly and quietly I sensed a harmony of life I had never known. I was experiencing the dawn of creation and could hear God's affirmation of its goodness. "...and it was so...and God saw that it was good." I did too.

In the gentle rhythms and melodies of life we know without fail that sense of harmony. It is the interconnectedness of all things, in perfect balance. It seems to defy description.

At times in my life, I have felt that perfect balance within myself; a balance of mind, body and spirit. When this happens, I can be fully present in relationships with family and friends.

I discovered this at the end of a year of teaching at Valparaiso University. It had been a rough year. We had three small children. A student we had befriended approached us during finals and said, "I don't have anything to do between finals and graduation. You two take off and I'll stay with your kids."

It was so unexpected, so full of grace. We often talk about the harmony we felt during those four days, traveling side roads and going nowhere in particular. We didn't know how stressed our lives were, separately and as a couple, until we stepped out of our normal routine. It made such a strong impression on us that we've done it ever since, taking three or four days just to be with each other and experience the oneness that God intended for us.

The harmony we treasure in nature, within ourselves and in our relationships with others pales when we reflect on the harmony we experience in relation to God.

My last sabbatical year was at Stanford University. I decided to spend a week of that time at Esalen, a magnificent retreat center at Big Sur on the coast of California. It was a wonderful week of interesting workshops, delightful people and nature at its best. I couldn't imagine anything topping what I experienced that week.

On my way home, I remembered this was the week of the internationally known Bach festival at Carmel. I decided to stop and see if by some long shot, I might get in on the performance of Bach's B Minor Mass that Sunday afternoon.

I got there five minutes before the performance and was told that the performance had been sold out for months, but that somebody had just turned in a ticket. The seat was 10 rows from the front in the very center of the auditorium. I thought the week before had been a rich spiritual experience,

but as I listened to Bach's magnificent expression of faith through what is perhaps the greatest musical composition ever written, I knew, as never before, where my faith was grounded.

During this one performance, I decided this was the music I wanted to be listening to in the hour of my dying. This, more than anything else, makes me sure that nothing, not even death, can separate me from the love of God in Christ. Amen!

Your experiences of harmony will likely not be the same as mine. There is such a richness of diversity in God's creation; no two of us are alike. But we all have a need for harmony and balance in our lives.

This harmony cannot be forced anymore than we can force someone to love us. What we can do is work to control the conditions that prevent harmony and balance in our lives; overwork, ignoring relationships, stress, busyness and ignoring our spiritual needs. God created us to be in harmony with Him and all of creation. When we are gifted with such experiences we have a foretaste of the life to come— when harmony will be the rule, not the exception, and we will be filled with the peace of God which passes all understanding.

Age Knows No Limit

James Cagney

Surely the vital thing in old age is to maintain an interest in and never stop planning for the future. I started painting at sixty and am still intensely caught up in it. I am studying classical guitar and I've also just taken up the bugle, trying to learn all the traditional carriage calls. For my physical well-being, I still put on a record and do a chorus or two of buck dancing. It's a mistake to set limits on yourself; life will do that whether you like it or not. A successful life must be determined by one's attitude. In a favorite phrase of my brother Ed, "We live between our ears." Sermon over.

My Life's History

Grandma Moses

What a strange thing is memory, and hope; one looks backward, the other forward. The one is of today, the other is the Tomorrow. Memory is history recorded in our brain, memory is a painter, it paints pictures of the past and of the day...

If I didn't start painting, I would have raised chickens. I could still do it now. I would never sit back in a rocking chair, waiting for someone to help me. I have often said, before I would call for help from outsiders, I would rent a room in the city some place and give pancake suppers, just pancake and syrup, and they could have water, like a little breakfast. I never dreamed that the pictures would bring in so much, and as for all that publicity, and as for the fame which came to Grandma so late, that I am too old to care for now. Sometimes it makes me think of a dream that my father once told at the breakfast table one morning many years ago. He said, "I had a dream about you last night, Anna Mary." "Was it good or bad, Pa?" And he said, "That depends on the future, dreams cast their shadows before us."

He dreamed, I was in a large hall and there were many people there, they were clapping their hands and shouting and he wondered what it was all about. "And looking I saw you, Anna Mary, coming my way, walking on the shoulders of men; you came right on stepping from one shoulder to another, waving to me." Of late years I have often thought of that dream, since all the publicity about me, and of my mother saying to father, "Now Russell, Anna Mary would look nice walking on men's shoulders!" She saw the folly of that dream. Or did that dream cast its shadows before? I often wonder, now that I am getting such kind well-wishing letters from almost every country on the globe...

Even now I am not old, I never think of it, yet I am a grandmother to eleven children, I also have seventeen great-grandchildren, that's aplenty!

Anna Mary Robertson ("Grandma") Moses, one of America's best known folk artists, began painting while in her seventies. Her works celebrate rural traditions and community life.

Grandma Moses at her painting table. 1952.
Photograph by Ifor Thomas. Copyright © 1990,
Grandma Moses Properties, Co., New York

Unanswered Prayer

Elise Maclay

How satisfying it is
On this gray November day
To brew pot after pot of coffee
While I pursue
My own projects
At my own pace
In my own way.
Anyone I want or need to talk to
Is as near as the phone.
On the other hand,
Working alone
I get more done.
Have more ideas.
My time is not taken up with meetings,
Office politics, polite greetings.

Even the much touted
　Support system
　　I had as an executive—
　　　Secretary, file clerk, switchboard operator—
　　　　Got in the way of the
　　　　　Free-wheeling creativity
　　　　　That sparks my day
　　　　　Now that I'm retired.
　　　　　　I never dreamed it would be
　　　　　　Like this.
　　　　　　　Ideas tumbling one over the other.
　　　　　　　I thought I'd sink in unstructured time.
　　　　　　　Instead, I'm just beginning to see
　　　　　　　　What a lead weight the routine of an office can be.
　　　　　　　Oh God, thank you
　　　　　　　For not listening
　　　　　　　　When I begged you not to let them
　　　　　　　　Retire me.

Where There is Humor, There is Hope

Where there is humor, there is hope. It's been said that laughter is the best medicine. Why? Because laughter not only helps us see the world in a positive light, but it actually impacts our physical health and well-being, as well.

As we age, we learn to enjoy and appreciate the little things in life. To see the humor in things that surround us. Maybe it's that we come to realize that we can't afford to take life—or ourselves—too seriously. That life truly is too short.

For it is through humor and laughter that we can wash away loneliness...fear...pain. Through laughter, we see a beacon of light...a flicker of hope even as we endure the most difficult of life's situations.

It is through humor that we can accept the changes along life's journey...and truly live life to the fullest.

"Rejoice in the Lord always. I will say it again; Rejoice!"

Philippians 4:4 NIV

"Twenty sit-ups start the day."
Pearl Swiggum,
newspaper author, age 80.

Aging: It's Good for a Laugh

Pearl Swiggum

Growing old has been double trouble as I've gone from afraid I will to afraid I won't and back, starting young. A lot of time has flown by between "Oh dear, how fast the years are going," to now at 80: "There may not be many left so hallelujah, let's have fun."

Back when I was eight, aging didn't look like anything I would enjoy. The adults in my small world hardly ever laughed. I saw a few men do so sometimes but didn't know why. Farmers from around our village tied their teams in front of our general store, gathered around the pot-bellied stove winter or summer, talked and chuckled.

Eavesdropping behind the counter—which I did a lot trying to learn what grownups said when there were no children around— was useless. Years later, I figured out why our father, no matter how we begged, refused to teach us Norwegian.

Women took life seriously. They all wore drab cotton dresses with slips and voluminous bloomers (we kids always checked the neighbors' clotheslines) under them, big aprons over all, and frowns. All except one.

I begged constantly to be allowed to go home from school and spend the night with one classmate. The attraction—their farm and her mother. Once a younger brother came from the shed where he had been shooting at pigeons. Their mother turned her back, bent over and presented a broad target. He shot. The pellet plopped harmlessly against her many layers of clothing and she laughed.

Because of her antics and probably because she laughed so much it was whispered around that she was a couple of eggs short of a clutch. That, even if it had been true, was unimportant. I loved her and hoped that if I should ever grow so old (she was about 40) I would have as much fun.

As I grew up, my desperate dream was to have a family of my own, a home of my own on a farm and a farmer for a husband. It all came true. Not in that order. And as our life evolved, I turned into a jealous, possessive mother.

Baby-sitting wasn't known at that time. Nobody got to take care of my children unless it was impossible to get out of going somewhere that they could not be taken along. When that happened there were two other young mothers in the clan and we cared for each others' children, never more than a few hours. Sort of a speedy cousin round robin.

And aging again loomed large. I was afraid I wouldn't. Obsessed with not being around to see my children grow—my mother died when I was three and I was probably a little manic on the subject—I wrote things on the backs of pictures like: "This is your mother wading in the creek with you"..."Your mother took this picture of you making mud pies"..."Here is your mother milking a cow. She is the one on the stool." I lie. I didn't add that last sentence.

Today if I could go back and live over any part of my life it would be those years. And I would laugh more. Did I help them to have fun? They assure me that I did. Small comfort.

I, myself, taught them that if the truth may hurt, then lie.

It is a puzzle. How did I arrive at this stage of life, accepting that it is the last; contented, a little slow and stiff but patient with it; getting every bit of enjoyment out of every day? I don't know. But I see on the faces of my peers the very same. Call it happiness.

The children I worried about so are grown and gone. Maybe this felicitous stage of my life began when they turned into my parents: "Mother, go have your flu shot." And "Mother, stay home today. The roads are icy."

While loving their concern, I do draw the line sometimes. I have become Lewis Carroll's Old Father William when he responded to his son's insistence that he was old and should act his age: "Be off or I'll kick you downstairs."

Maybe this pleasurable time began when milking machines were invented, when jeans spelled the end of climbing over fences in a house dress, when Social Security was born. Maybe the uncountable, sometimes incomprehensible inventions have infused us with "what next?" anticipation while not diminishing "wait and see" patience.

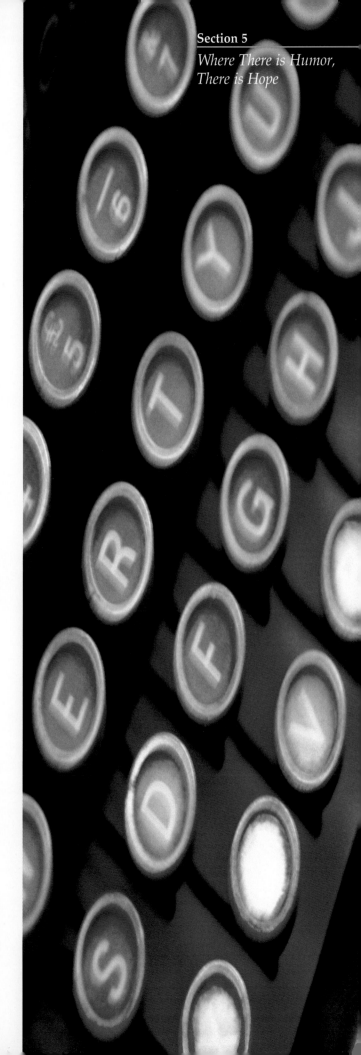

Whatever the reason for our happy old age, we each have a list, probably unspoken, of contributing factors. Here is mine:

Pearl's Wisdom

Buy everything that you want, no matter how frivolous, that you have money to pay for.

Write about your childhood. Make copies.

If you forget something don't fret. Forget that you forgot it.

If you live alone talk to somebody every day.

Don't be set in your ways. Sometimes eat ice cream for breakfast. Or clam dip.

Drink prune juice.

Write a letter every day. Good for the person who gets it and also good for you.

There will be crying. Be sure to laugh more.

Walk every day. Indoors or out.

Hang onto railings.

Paint over the lower two-thirds of the big bathroom mirror. That is the only one on the list that I haven't done. But I have the paint.

Some Signs That Old Age Might Be Creeping Up On You

George Burns

When you like to be in crowds because they keep you from falling down.

When the parts that have the arthritis are the parts where you feel the best.

When your favorite section of the newspaper is "25 Years Ago Today."

When a big evening with your friends is sitting around comparing living wills.

When your knees buckle and your belt won't.

When your clothes go into the overnight bag so you can fill the suitcase with your pills.

When your idea of a change of scenery is looking to the left or right.

When somebody you consider an old-timer calls you an old-timer.

"Be Healthy – Try Laughter"

Win Arn

*"A cheerful heart
is good medicine."*

-Solomon

For centuries, the value of laughter and positive emotions have been known to contribute to the health, healing and happiness of people. Scripture records that a "cheerful heart is good medicine." (Proverbs 15:13) So it is today that older adults – or anyone else who desires to live long and love it – will want to keep a twinkle in their eye and a merry heart.

To be able to laugh at oneself, at the foolishness of the world, at problems, to laugh when things aren't funny – that is a secret of those who enjoy a long and happy life. There is healing in humor.

Happiness and other positive emotions produce positive effects in the body. Many scientists believe that hearty laughter helps the human brain produce natural pain killers and helps to release the full range of positive emotions.

Humor is physically, mentally, and emotionally therapeutic.

But how can we cultivate a sense of humor—and start reaping some of the benefits of a lighter, more laughter-filled life? Here are some suggestions:

Step 1: Expose yourself to good humor.

There are plenty of good humorous books that make for enjoyable reading in your evening hours. Or, if you hear of a famous comedian coming to your area, buy some tickets and go enjoy a good laugh.

Step 2: Do something silly.

We tend to lose one of the wonderful joys of childhood as we move into the self-conscious years of adolescence, and many people don't ever get it back. It's the fun of being silly. Your assignment for this step is to go do something silly. It's more fun when you do it with other people, rather than hidden behind a locked door. But if it helps, you can try a few silly things there first. Don't worry about your reputation. If anything it will improve!

**Step 3: Laugh out loud,
whether you feel like it or not.**

Hearing yourself laugh actually causes you to laugh even more. Try it right now. Just start laughing out loud. Then listen to yourself. Pretty soon you will be laughing at your own laughing! If you think that's funny, try getting three or four of your friends together and do the same thing. Tell the group that on the count of three you are all going to start laughing. Before you know it, you'll be rolling in the aisles. The next time you hear or see something funny, laugh out loud. Don't just smile or chuckle. Laugh!

Step 4: Tell one funny story each day for the next two weeks.

See if you can get one person to laugh aloud each day at something humorous you share. If you're telling a joke, practice it beforehand to get the greatest impact. And be sure, when you finish the punch line, to enjoy it and laugh at the joke yourself. Pretend it is the first time you've heard it.

Are you ready to laugh? Here are a few amusing anecdotes...enjoy them just for the health of it!

102nd Birthday

A newspaper reporter asked a lady who was celebrating her 102nd birthday, what was the best thing about being 102. She replied, "The absence of peer pressure!"

Third Husband

An older gentleman had recently entered a retirement center. During his first meal in the dining room, he noticed a lady across the table staring intently at him. Finally, it became so embarrassing he asked her, "Why are you staring at me?" "Oh, I'm sorry," she replied, "It's just that you look like my third husband." "Is that right? And how many husbands have you had?" he inquired. Her reply - "Two."

Young and Swift... Old and Rich

It was during the holiday shopping time, stores were crowded, parking was difficult. An older lady in her Mercedes had driven around the parking lot again and again, looking for a place. Finally, she spotted a car preparing to back out. Just before she could pull into the spot, a red sports car zoomed around her and took the spot. The young driver, as he walked past her, called out, "That's the way it is when you are young and swift."

As the young man continued to walk away, the older lady stepped on her accelerator and rammed the back end of the expensive sports car. A loud crash caused the young man to turn and see the older lady as she called out, "That's the way it is when you are old and rich."

Remember, "A cheerful heart is good medicine." Have a good laugh today and then share it with someone else. You'll both be healthier and happier for the experience!

How Old Am I?

Lee Meriwether

Age is a quality of mind;
If you have left your dreams behind;
If hope is lost;
If you no longer look ahead;
If your ambitions are dead;
You are old.

But if from Life you take the best;
If in Life you keep the jest,
If Love you hold,
No matter how the years go by,
No matter how the birthdays fly,
You are not old.

A Philosophy On Aging

Phyllis Diller

We have to be philosophical about life. Things could always be worse. It's all a matter of values. I have a needle-point motto hanging in my breakfast nook.

*When World War III
Is On The Horizon
Don't Sweat
The Kitchen Scuff Marks*

This was put up there by my housekeeper who hates to clean scuff marks.

I have since volunteered her name on the women's draft.

If we tried we could always find something to worry ourselves silly about. Especially me. My life is a series of regrets and ponderables. I call them "ifs."

* If I were a perfect "10" (instead of a cumulative 10—five parts of me are rated "2")...

* If I hadn't caused that disturbance at Baskin-Robbins by asking for a thirty-second flavor...

* If I never got that kidney transplant from a bedwetter...

If, if, if, if.

We all have regrets but we can't keep wallowing in self-pity.

The healthiest thing you can do is feel GOOD about yourself. Forget the fact that you may be a total mess (some of us can't help it...we were born with the gene for "total messiness").

Be like the girl singer who was on a variety show with me. She had a wig, capped teeth, false eyelashes, fake fingernails, rear padding and a silicone job. She then went out on stage and sang, "I Gotta Be Me."

The Search for Spiritual Meaning

Throughout our lives, we are often too caught up in the daily hustle and bustle to really take a close look at what we're all about.

As we age, our perspective changes. Things that were once important may seem rather insignificant. We realize that the true meaning of our lives doesn't come from fancy cars, vacations or trendy clothes. It's something far less tangible. And far more priceless.

Through the years, we realize that the real treasure in life is fulfilling our never-ending quest for inner peace... knowing that through the ups and downs we face along life's journey, our Christian faith is what makes us strong...and helps us endure.

That's the beauty of aging. It's having the ability to put life in perspective. To enjoy a time of reflection. To have the inner strength to handle challenges and the wisdom to face life with dignity.

Just as life is a journey...in a constant state of transition, so too, is our relationship with God. As we age, we realize that the grace of God is what really matters in life.

> "Since we have been justified through faith, we have peace with God through our Lord Jesus Christ."
>
> Romans 5:1 NIV

Life's Journey

Oswald C.J. Hoffmann

You know that you are getting old when you attend more funerals than you do weddings. I don't mind attending funerals of people my own age. It hurts to attend the funeral of someone who has died in the bloom of manhood or womanhood—younger people in their 20s or 30s!

Grief is human. In fact, it is all too human. It brings up feelings of guilt about things you or other people could have done and did not do—and about things you perhaps did and should not have done.

We all have experiences we regret. It's been said, "Regret is the stuff of which life is made." One who has no regrets has not lived at all.

With regrets, and also the guilt that follows, there comes grace. It comes not out of our own souls or from the gracious comments of others, but directly from the heart of God. Now God is in the picture. But, he was there all along, sometimes unrecognized.

There was a lot of guilt the day the Son of God died for the sins of the world. Some of it was quiet, and some of it was blatant! That's the way guilt is. The more you try to cover it up, the noisier it gets. And noise is something that is not becoming to age, old or otherwise. A real mark of maturity in old age is the ability to observe, to reflect, and to encourage—without dredging up old wrongs or assuming a "know-it-all" attitude.

Age reminds people of things they did when they did not really know what they were doing. To many people, age is a reminder of misdeeds when they were young, and of failures when they grew older. Some of those things happened only the day before yesterday: unkind words, unhealthy actions, selfish desires, an ungenerous spirit, and a readiness to offend which are often the marks not so much of the younger generation as of the older generation.

If I read the Word of God correctly, it is forgiveness that makes old age the golden age. Those who have learned the grace of God's forgiveness and also the art of forgiving one another, are the salt of the earth. They are the light of the world. They hold forth a helping hand to those who need it, just as the Lord held out his helping hand to all who need that hand.

There is no doubt about the problems of age. One has to be impressed, however, with the authentic faith of people who know the Lord Jesus Christ and the power of His resurrection. People like that have already left their families and friends a tremendous inheritance, a genuine treasure.

If I had any personal advice to give to people my own age, and of every age, I would say, "Get a good grip on Christ, and keep on handing down with a smile the Good News of His resurrection from the dead." That bequest will be long remembered!

Homily for Myself

Charles J. Fahey

I celebrated my 60th birthday this past April. For one who often writes and speaks theoretically about the "Third Age," how does it really feel to be into it? While there is nothing magical about The Big Six O, it has created an understanding in my heart as well as my mind that I have entered the latter part of life. This has come as something of a jolt and, I hope, as a moment of grace.

For many years I have proclaimed that inertia, distraction and denial are the enemies of the third age. They should be replaced by reflection, honesty about one's capacities and deliberate decisions.

NOT THAT OLD?

I think of 60-year-olds and say to myself, "I am not that old." How ageist, how much denial, how wrong. The reality is that I have declining, yet substantial physical capacities that I can maximize and, to some extent, conserve—but only with deliberate action.

I formally entered the field of aging in 1961. It seems like yesterday. Recently, I have become aware that few of those active in the field then are alive today. Indeed many who became active subsequent to that period have retired and many others have died. I find that I have become one of the veterans!

I am experiencing an increased urgency to use time well. This is coupled with a certain sense of freedom: I am who I am for better or worse. This reflection is hardly morbid; it is one of realism, the beginning of wisdom.

Paul Baltes, the distinguished psychologist at the University of Berlin, speaks of how we continually adapt throughout the life course. He says that the process of selection within life's limits and the ways in which we optimize our choices and compensate for our losses are particularly important aspects of "successful aging."

In addition to, and perhaps even more important than resolutions about the physical side of my aging process, there are other things on which I want to concentrate my psychic energies: being a better friend, being more hospitable and being a more wise and courageous moral leader in the social institutions central to my life.

The third age should be a time of maturity in relationships. I know that I should be more committed and skilled in relating to people, both those I have known and those who are strangers. The human heart has a great capacity and a need to love well. The third age should be a period in which the skills developed in a lifetime of relationships come to fruition.

In addition to my family, the social structures that have influenced me are primarily the church, our country and the field of aging. Each has goodness and each is flawed; each has rich traditions, but each needs to understand more fully and act more in accord with evolving knowledge. Each has been good to me, and each deserves the benefit of whatever knowledge and experience I have gained in my 60 years.

The past six decades have been filled with surprises; some good and some bad, and I am sure whatever years the Lord affords me will be filled with more. It is good to know that whatever happens to me will also be shared with the communities—in particular the field of aging—about which I care and which care about me.

When God Began In The Middle

Joseph John Juknialis

The God in whom we believe
is a God who comes into our lives
from beginning to end.

He comes as life unfolds,
threading a seam between winter and spring.

He is present in moments of death,
harvesting the fruits of our autumns.

But most frequently he comes into the middle of life,
in the summer of our days.

He comes into the midst of success and of failure,
into fear as well as into comfort.

He makes himself known in moments of grace
and in moments of sin,
in love
and in loneliness.

It is in the middle of our lives
that we come to realize what faith means
and what it demands.

It is in the middle of our lives
that love is redefined,
that the seeds of wisdom are sown,
that we begin to surrender control over our lives
to a force greater than ourselves.

Those who have journeyed the middle of life
carry with them
forever
the memories of times
When God Began In The Middle.

When You Get There, Wait

Walter Wangerin, Jr.

Little one, are you afraid of the dark?

Is that why you grab my hand and press against me? Because you are frightened?

Little one, you whimper with fear. You turn and you bury your face in my bosom. I hug you with all my strength, with all my love. I rock you and rock you and stroke your thin hair – but still you are scared of the dark.

O little one, we know what your darkness is, don't we?

It's old age. You have grown old. And now comes the deepest darkness of all: you are dying.

My little one, my darling! The dark is your departure. You are leaving this world altogether, going to that undiscovered country from whose bourn no traveler returns. Yes? Yes.

Yes, and my darkness is sorrow, because I must remain behind.

Hush, old hoary head. My best beloved, hush. Let me hold you a while. Cling to me as tightly as you please, and I will whisper the thoughts that occur to me now.

No. This is not some city through which we travel. Yet there is a city ahead of you. And you shall enter before I do. But I am coming, and then it shall be you who welcomes me and makes the streets of that place familiar to me.

Because you are dying in faith, my little one – you who always were but a pilgrim on this earth. You're finishing the trip begun by baptism; you are entering a better country, that is, a heavenly country. Whereof God is not ashamed to be called your God – for he hath prepared for you this city!

And when you arrive, you won't need me to show you around. God will meet you there. Alleys and highways, God will show you everything – but first he'll take from your vision the crust of old age, the terrors and the troubles of this present world: for God himself shall wipe all tears from your eyes; and there shall be no more death neither sorrow, nor crying anymore.

And no: the dark surrounding you now is not the countryside either, nor sky nor stars nor the woofings and bleats of God's creatures. It is, in fact, their absence, since you are passing away from all this.

Ah, but you go from creation to its Creator! You go to the God who conceived of Eden and Paradise and everything between the two. Better than the handiwork of God, dear heart, is God himself.

But yes: dying is a kind of blindness. It is preparation for deeper sight and dearest insight. Little one, this darkness is not because you cannot see, but because the world cannot be seen. The material world is becoming a shadow before you, so that the coming world (bright with divine reality) may not blind you at arrival. That city is brighter than sunlight. It hath no need of the sun in it. For the glory of God doth lighten it, and the Lamb is the light thereof.

Hush now. Close your eyes. Don't be afraid. I'll hold you with my lowly love till God receives you in his highest, most holy love. My darling, you are embarking through darkness on your best adventure. Only the start is scary. The rest is endlessly marvelous, eternally beautiful.

But when you get there, wait!

Turn around. Look back through the glorious light, and watch for me. I am coming too.

Moving Closer
to the Heart

Burl Ives

About twenty years ago I began asking questions: Who am I? Where am I going? What is the significance of life? What is my purpose here on earth? Those are the sorts of questions that captured my attention. I became more and more introspective. So I'm less social now and more philosophical about life than when I was younger.

Material things have become increasingly less important to me as I've aged, while spiritual things have become more important. I remember back in 1946 when I ran into tax problems and had to sell my home and four-acre property here in California. Friends came to me weeping, telling me that this was a terrible thing. But I recognized even then that the house and the land were really only on loan to me, that a man isn't here long enough to truly say that he owns anything. So I just said to my friends, "I'm just passing through. Don't fret about this; something else will come along." I lost something that appeared to be very important in order to gain something far more significant.

I think my life has been a long, slow process of trying to move closer and closer to the heart.

"He is no fool

who gives

what he cannot keep,

to gain

what he cannot lose"

Jim Elliot

A Heart of Wisdom

hat is wisdom? It's not having read the most books or received the most degrees. Wisdom is the ability to share one's life experiences...to accept what is..to reflect without regret on what could have been...and to strive for what can be.

Wisdom is finding an inner peace and sharing that insight...that rare vision with others, so they, too, may see.

Wisdom is learning to live without regret...and knowing that all of life's disappointments, pleasures, pains and joys are a lifelong course in character building. Wisdom is learning from mistakes and celebrating life's triumphs. It is using life's experiences to gain an understanding of ourselves and our world. But to be of real value our wisdom must be shared.

True wisdom comes to us as a gift of God to be shared and celebrated with all generations.

"Teach us to number our days aright, that we may gain a heart of wisdom."

Psalm 90:12 NIV

A Heart of Wisdom

Martin Marty

"Just two months ago you passed your complete medical examination with flying colors. Why do you want a heart test now?" asked the physician.

"Because I want to take swimming lessons at the 'Y' and they demand word from my doctor that my heart is healthy."

"You? You're seventy years old! Why do you want to start to learn to swim at your age?" he asked.

"Oh, because last year my mother learned how, and she's been bugging me ever since!"

That is a story about the generations. I have no doubt you will tell it to others. Had I said: "You are never too old to learn!" or "Don't let anyone of any age put you down for your age!" your eyes would have glazed over and you would quickly have forgotten the point.

Stories are hard to forget. We use them to transact between generations, to help find meaning in our own lives, and to become more fully human.

Here are a few of my favorites:

Three old friends sitting on a park bench in the sun, visiting until sunset and its chill. They are not talking about the principles of life. They are telling stories of their young years, or about their grandchildren. They laugh, they cry, they become open to new experiences.

A widow and a widower, now in well-seasoned love, take walks. Does she ask him "by what ten principles do you live?" No, they ask and talk about their travels; she tells a story of abuse, or earlier love, or the children who might become his stepchildren. They share the stories to learn to know each other, to trust.

A friend is ill, terminally. You are busy. But something in you asks, "What am I doing today that is more important than visiting that friend? What will be more important to her than to tell me a story—not necessarily about the illness, though it may be healing to do so, but about what has happened through the years?" Through story I become part of the patient's world, and honor her suffering and faith.

It is family reunion time. Not everyone likes everyone. Late afternoon, after the ice cream melts and the coffee chills, someone at the picnic will complain about someone else who got grandmother's amethyst. Others will wonder to whom you will leave a particular cedar chest, or will talk about the black sheep of your cousin's family. But you would not miss the reunion for anything. If you are not there, the stories might be about you, behind your back. You will be there because through all the conflict that families have, they also tell stories that produce laughs, and tears.

One advantage of aging is that we gain more and longer stories, to make us human. One disadvantage, they tell us—but who would believe them?—is that we may tell more and more stories and they take longer and longer.

To say that we age well with stories does not mean that we have to talk only about ourselves. Grandparents who are veterans of World War II may find it egotistic or painful to make themselves the center of the story. But they can tell of how things were. In that way, stories are more than a form of communication. They are at the very heart of our wisdom. Wisdom we can and should share with others. Wisdom that will stand the test of time.

*"Wisdom is
meaningless
until our own
experience
has given it
meaning..."*

Bergen Evans

A Time to Remember

Melvin Kimble

Memories are not simply something we have; memories are what we are.

Sharing your life story is a marvelous gift not only to others, but also to yourself. By recalling past events you see the connections and events separated by time make sense. Memory is the thread that connects time and weaves a fabric of meaning. The fabric is a mosaic, but by reviewing our life story we find the patterns. Thus we find meaning for the present.

The gift of memory makes life review possible. And what riches we discover!

Perhaps the greatest value of sharing our memories is that it provides a legacy we can leave to others. This is an heirloom we share before we die. And in the act of sharing we profit both ourselves and our heirs.

Ah, but memory is imperfect. It is flawed. Some memories may be blocked out or covered by the grains of more recent harvest. We all need help especially to recall the emotions and thoughts that accompanied the events of the past. Because life review is more than a sentimental journey back through time we want to recall these also.

But the storehouse of memory can be primed. Rehearsing experiences can often unlock hidden memories. Old photos or mementos can surface memories of events and experiences long "forgotten." But the best aid to memory is a good listener—someone with whom a person can share the story of his or her life.

This is a role anyone can play whether five or ninety-five. It means gently nudging persons to reflect on joyful or sorrowful events in their lives and what they meant. Asking for more, asking for feelings and learnings, these are the threads that bring out the patterns of meaning. Listening is the gift we give to those who give us the gift of their life review.

The reviewing and telling of one's life story has many functions.

It assists people in becoming aware of the continuity and meaning of life. It helps reveal God's presence in our lives. And, it helps us come to terms with the lives we have lived.

We do not merely have these memories, we are these memories.

Older and Wiser

Ossie Davis

From experience, I would say that age is the point of elevation from which it is easier to see who you are, what it is you want to do, and from which you find yourself closer to the very center of the universe. Living through many changes, through many years, seeing many public passions rise and fall, gives you a sense of continuity. And that continuity not only is a part of your own view, but it also attaches itself to the continuity of time altogether. So I can look back and see way back, but somehow that enables me to look forward and see way forward. Age makes knowledge, tempers knowledge with experience, and out of that comes the possibility of wisdom. We never know if we're truly wise.

I question wisdom now as much as I ever did. I'm not content to tell you that now that I'm old, I'm wise. It is not that I am not in some instances wise or don't appreciate wisdom, it is just that none of our knowledge is set; it changes from moment to moment. It is the person who continually questions his wisdom who has a remote chance of someday becoming wise.

So the aged are not necessarily wise, but chances are they are wiser than the young. And this is why I feel the world now needs us as it's never needed us before. In this age of rapid change in technology, somebody has to say, "Whoa, technology can only affect reality; it cannot give you what should be, only change what is." Who's going to tell technology what should be? The people who've had more experience, and to have experience means you have lived through things.

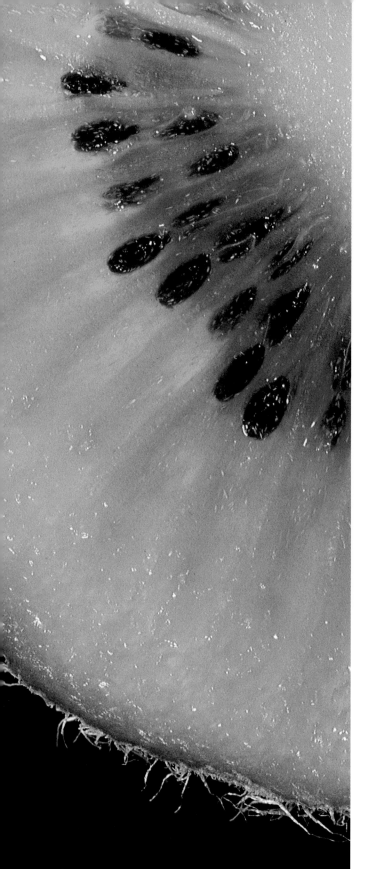

"We are not yet what we shall be, but we are growing toward it"

Martin Luther

Living to a Ripe Age

Hugh Downs

I don't know what it will take to turn around the American attitude. When will we finally understand that the older a person is, the more of a monument one is to what's worthwhile in life? Because all the forces that try to pull us down and destroy us in our cribs and through our childhood and through our mid-life are immense. If you survive those things, we still tend to put you in the same basket as decrepitude and impairment, which is not only unfair, it's kind of silly.

The way I see it, I finally got it together. It took me a long time, you know. Wouldn't it be nice if at twenty-five you had all the accumulated wisdom and acquired techniques that you later get? It just almost never happens. It makes me think that if I could contrive to live to be 400 years old, I really would have it down, wouldn't I? But you wouldn't suddenly want to become seventy years old, any more than you would really want to remain twenty. You know, there's an anomaly in our youth-oriented "Pepsi Generation" mentality. People say, "Well, what I'd like to have is the wisdom I now have, but in a twenty-year-old body." I think that's an anomaly because, first of all, to be twenty you would have to have the whole ball game – you know, the ignorance, the uncertainty. The other thing about being older is that I won't get killed in World War II – I already made it through that. I wouldn't want to try it a second time around.

You know, a man who was celebrated for his extremely good judgment was once asked, "How did you get so much good judgment?" And the man said, "Through experience." And then he was asked, "How did you come by the experience?" And the man said, "Through bad judgment." So that actually when you make mistakes, if you learn from them, that's fine. There is such a thing as getting in a kind of a rut where you keep repeating the same mistakes – you know, the compulsive, repetitive mistakes. That's a psychological problem; a normal person, I think, learns from mistakes. And I learned from mistakes right down the line —

mistakes in career, mistakes in marriage — until I was finally able to say, "Boy, I'm out of that trap. Now I know the right technique."

Both Socrates and Freud stressed the importance of knowing yourself, because if you've got an awful lot of makeup underneath a level of personality that you aren't conscious of, then you've got dichotomy — you've got parts of yourself working against yourself. The more you know yourself, the more whole you are and the more comfortable you are and the more mature you are in the best sense of the word "mature." Not everybody matures, and that's sad. There are plenty of people who live to be quite old who don't mature. I liken it to a piece of fruit. You can go from green to rotten without ever ripening, and that's tragic. And there are humans that that happens to, so its important to mature, to ripen. I suppose that's what I hope for myself — that I continue to ripen until it's my time to go.

If I Had My Life To Live Over

Nadine Stair

I'd dare to make more mistakes next time. I'd relax, I would limber up. I would be sillier than I have been on this trip. I would take fewer things seriously. I would take more chances. I would climb more mountains and swim more rivers. I would eat more ice cream and less beans. I would perhaps have more actual troubles, but I'd have fewer imaginary ones.

You see, I'm one of those people who live sensibly and sanely hour after hour, day after day. Oh, I've had my moments, and if I had it to do over again, I'd have more of them. In fact, I'd try to have nothing else. Just moments, one after another, instead of living so many years ahead of each day. I've been one of those persons who never goes any-where without a thermometer, a hot water bottle, a raincoat and a parachute. If I had to do it again, I would travel lighter than I have.

If I had my life to live over, I would start barefoot earlier in the spring and stay that way later in the fall. I would go to more dances. I would ride more merry-go-rounds. I would pick more daisies.

Contributors

DR. CHARLES ARN is president of Church Growth, Inc., Monrovia, CA & co-author of three popular books on aging, including *Catch the Age Wave*.

DR. WIN ARN has authored eleven books, produced thirty films/videos and is an international lecturer. He serves as President of Living In Full Effectiveness (L.I.F.E.) and New Senior Study Center.

REV. HERB BROKERING has, since 1970, served as a freelance educator, writer and pastor at large, providing consultation across the United States, Japan and Europe. He has authored 33 books including, *I Opener*, *Wholly Holy*, *Lord If*, *The Night Before Jesus*, *Surprise Me Jesus* and *Pilgrimage to Renewal*. He conducts small group pilgrimages to eastern Germany, Poland, the Czech Republic, Slovakia, Hungary and Israel. For the past 25 years he has been adjunct Professor at Luther Seminary, St. Paul, Minnesota.

REV. THOMAS A. DROEGE, MA, Ph.D. is a Lutheran pastor and educator whose area of expertise is health and spirituality. After a career of teaching and research in practical theology at Valparaiso University, he joined the Interfaith Health Resources Center as Associate Director in 1992 and has authored several books and articles on the subject of faith development studies, understanding death and dying, and health and spirituality.

MSGR. CHARLES FAHEY is a Senior Associate at Fordham University's Third Age Center and is the Marie Ward Doty Professor of Aging Studies at the university. As a public speaker, he has worked as an advocate to improve the long-term care and housing for the elderly. He has played a major role in stimulating and helping religious groups to be more aware of the issues of aging. He is president of the American Society on Aging.

GRACIA GRINDAL is a Professor of Rhetoric at Luther Seminary. Her interests lie in uncovering the connection between theology, culture and hymnody. She has authored several publications and original hymns.

DR. OSWALD C.J. HOFFMANN is widely recognized as an outstanding Protestant church leader and was awarded the Wittenberg National Clergy Award from Luther Institute in Washington, D.C. in 1993. He has authored several books and articles, including *Hurry Home Where You Belong*, *God Is No Island*, *Life Crucified*, *The Lord's Prayer* and *There Is Hope*. He has appeared on numerous network television and radio programs and served over 33 years as speaker on "The Lutheran Hour", a world-wide religious radio program, produced by The International Lutheran Layman's League, an auxilliary of The Lutheran Church—Missouri Synod.

JO HORNE's experience with issues of aging has come from authoring four books for caregivers, managing the care of her own parents, founding an adult daycare center and working for the long-term care division of a major national insurance company. She is a recognized expert on the issue of giving care and has appeared on national television and radio talk programs.

DR. MELVIN A. KIMBLE, Ph.D. is a Professor of Pastoral Theology and Ministry and Director of the Center for Aging, Religion and Spirituality at Luther Seminary, St. Paul, Minnesota. He is an ordained pastor in the Evangelical Lutheran Church in America.

ART LINKLETTER's career in television and radio spans nearly five decades. He has performed in two of the longest running shows in broadcast history: *House Party* on CBS-TV and radio for 25 years and *People Are Funny*, on NBC-TV and radio for 19 years. He won one Emmy award and was nominated for several others. He has also appeared in several television specials, television dramas and two major motion pictures. He has authored 23 publications, including *Kids Say the Darndest Things* which is one of the top 15 best sellers in American publishing history. He holds 10 honorary doctorate degrees and has served on the President's National Advisory Council for Drug Abuse Prevention and on other national committees.

His most recent best-seller is *Old Age Is Not For Sissies*. He has just completed an assignment as Ambassador to Austrailia for their 150th birthday celebration.

REV. KARL LUTZE served on the staff of the Lutheran Human Relations Association of America for 21 years and taught part-time as a member of Valparaiso University's theology faculty. He is the author of two books, *To Mend the Broken* and *Forgive Our Forgettings, Lord*. He has served the larger Lutheran Community as charter member of the National Indian Lutheran Board; The Lutheran Church—Missouri Synod, as member of its Standing Committee on Human Care; and his own community as board member of PACT - "Prisoners And Community Together". He is the first executive director of the Association of Lutheran Older Adults, an inter-Lutheran ministry for people nearing or past 50 years of age.

DR. MARTIN E. MARTY is the Fairfax M. Cone Distinguished Service Professor at The University of Chicago. He is Senior Editor of the weekly The Christian Century, author of the newsletter Context, coeditor of the quarterly Church History and founding president of the Park Ridge Center for the Study of Health, Faith and Ethics. He holds 52 honorary degrees and is Chairman of the Board of Regents of St. Olaf College.

REV. JAMES P. SCHAEFER is retired after serving as parish pastor, director of public relations and stewardship for the Wisconsin Evangelical Lutheran Synod and later editor of its monthly magazine for the laity.

PEARL SWIGGUM writes a weekly column for the Gays Mills, Wisconsin Independent—a pursuit she began over 36 years ago. Today, the column is also published in The Wisconsin State Journal, another daily and several weekly newspapers. She has published a book, *Stump Ridge Farm*, a collection of her earlier and most treasured columns. The book is named for the farm on which she lives which has been in her family for more than 100 years.

Permissions

BURNS, GEORGE: "Some Signs That Old Age Might Be Creeping Up On You" Reprinted by permission of The Putnam Publishing Group from WISDOM OF THE 90's by George Burns. Copyright © 1991 by George Burns.

CAGNEY, JAMES: "Age Knows No Limit" Taken from *Cagney by Cagney*, J. Cagney. Copyright © 1976. Doubleday & Company, Inc. Garden City, NJ.

DAVIS, OSSIE: "Older and Wiser" Taken from "The Ageless Spirit", Copyright © 1992 by Phillip L. Berman and Connie Goldman. Published by Ballantine Books, a division of Random House, Inc., New York.

DELANY, SARAH & A. ELIZABETH: "Having Our Say: The Delany Sisters' First 100 Years" HAVING OUR SAY by Sarah and A. Elizabeth Delany with Amy Hill Hearth. Published in 1993 by Kodansha America, Inc. © by Amy Hill Hearth, Sarah Louise Delany and Annie Elizabeth Delany.

DILLER, PHYLLIS: "A Philosophy On Aging" Taken from *The Joys of Aging - and How to Avoid Them*, Copyright © 1981 by Phyllis Diller. Published by Doubleday & Company, Inc. Garden City, NJ.

DOWNS, HUGH: "Living to a Ripe Age" Taken from "The Ageless Spirit", Copyright © 1992 by Phillip L. Berman and Connie Goldman. Published by Ballantine Books, a division of Random House, Inc., New York.

FRANCIS, POLLY: "The Autumn of My Life" From "Songs of Experience", compiled and edited by Margaret Fowler and Priscilla McCutcheon. Published by Ballantine Books, New York. Every effort was made to clear permission and the publisher would welcome notice from the copyright holder.

HERBSTREIT, JUDY: "Dear Teri" From "Between Ourselves: Letters Between Mothers and Daughters, 1950-1982" by Judy Green Herbstreit. Published by Michael Joseph Ltd., London. Every effort was made to obtain permission and the publisher would welcome notice from the copyright holder.

IVES, BURL: "Moving Closer to the Heart" Taken from "The Ageless Spirit", Copyright © 1992 by Phillip L. Berman and Connie Goldman. Published by Ballantine Books, a division of Random House, Inc., New York.

JUKNIALIS, JOSEPH: "When God Began In The Middle" Reprinted from the preface of *When God Began In the Middle* by Joseph J. Juknialis. Copyright © 1982 by Resource Publications, Inc., 160 E. Virginia St. #290, San Jose, CA 95112.

KNOWLTON, MARTY: "Stir It Up" Taken from "The Ageless Spirit", Copyright © 1992 by Phillip L. Berman and Connie Goldman. Published by Ballantine Books, a division of Random House, Inc., New York.

MACLAY, ELISE: "Free" and "Unanswered Prayer" Reprinted by permission of the author.

MAY, ROLLO: "Creativity: A Fresh Approach to Aging" Taken from "The Ageless Spirit", Copyright © 1992 by Phillip L. Berman and Connie Goldman. Published by Ballantine Books, a division of Random House, Inc., New York.

MERIWETHER, LEE: "How Old Am I?" Lee Meriwether, *How Old Am I?*, reprinted with permission of Greenwood Publishing Group, Inc., Westport, CT. Copyright © 1991 by Belle Boone Beard Gerontology Center, Lynchburg College.

MOSES, GRANDMA: "My Life's History" Quote from Grandma Moses: *My Life's History* Copyright © 1952 (renewed 1980), Grandma Moses Properties, Co., New York.

SARTON, MAY: "At Seventy: A Journal" *From At Seventy: A Journal*, Copyright © 1984 by May Sarton. Printed in *Second Opinion*, Vol. 15. Reprinted with permission of the publisher, W.W. Norton & Co., Inc.

STAIR, NADINE: "If I Had My Life To Live Over" *If I Had My Life To Live Over*, by Nadine Stair. Used by permission of the publisher, Papier-Mache Press, Watsonville, CA.

SULLENDER, R. SCOTT: "Losses in Later Life" Used by permission of the publisher, Paulist Press, Mahwah, NJ.

WANGERIN, WALTER JR.: "When You Get There, Wait" Taken from the book, *Little Lamb, Who Made Thee?* by Walter Wangerin, Jr. Copyright © 1993 by Walter Wangerin, Jr. Used by permission of Zondervan Publishing House.

A one-hour audiocassette, based on "The Ageless Spirit", is available by contacting Connie Goldman Productions, 926 2nd St., Suite 201, Santa Monica, CA 90403. Write for information and cost.